How to Set Up a Work Area at Home for a Child with Autism

By: S. B. Linton
AutismClassroom.com

First Edition: January 2009

Table of Contents

Chapter 1

Introduction

Autism is a complex disability which affects individuals in the area of socialization, communication and behaviors. The CDC more specifically states this about autism:

"Autism spectrum disorders (ASDs) are a group of developmental disabilities defined by significant impairments in social interaction and communication and the presence of unusual behaviors and interests. Many people with ASDs also have unusual ways of learning, paying attention, or reacting to different sensations. The thinking and learning abilities of people with ASDs can vary – from gifted to severely challenged. ASD begins before the age of 3 and lasts throughout a person's life. It occurs in all racial, ethnic, and socioeconomic groups and is four times more likely to occur in boys than girls."

Behavior, communication and learning challenges can make educating a child with autism challenging at times. For some parents and caregivers, it is sometimes difficult to get their child to complete work tasks or homework. While our first AutismClassroom.com book How to Set Up a Classroom for Students with Autism, provides strategies for teachers and school based personnel, this book How to Set Up a Work Area at Home for a Child with Autism, intends to provide parents, family members and in-home support workers with a few ideas and strategies for home instruction. Some of the strategies are the same and some are tailored specifically for the home environment. As stated in the How to Set Up a Classroom for Student with Autism book, this book is a beginning step to a life-long learning process of teaching and learning. Please understand that there are so many other items that can be discussed which relate to autism and so much more to learn. However, this book is meant to put you on the "starting block" to creating an effective work area for your child. All of the ideas will not work for everyone, but please take what you can and use the strategies that work best for you and your family. This is only a beginning step. Enjoy.

-S. B. Linton

Chapter 2

Getting Started

Gathering the items mentioned in this chapter will depend on how detailed you would like your child's work area to be. Of course, you can create a work area without all of the items on this page, however, here are some ideas, to get you started. When thinking about your instruction at home, you may want to first compile a variety of materials.

- 1 box of sandwich size zipper baggies
- 1 box of gallon zipper baggies
- a permanent marker
- Velcro ™ dots (pre-cut) or Velcro strips
- heavy cardstock paper or foam board
- two 1/2 inch binders or 2-pocket folders
- dividers for binders
- a 3 hole punch device
- clear duct tape
- clear packing tape (to use as a quick laminator) or self-stick laminating sheets
- a pack of 8 x 11 inch paper
- white index cards small and large
- several clear containers with lids to store toys and work materials

The following furniture and room ideas may be helpful too:

- a child size desk or table
- appropriate sized chair (not too big or too small)
- a filing cabinet or bookshelf or large container
- a quiet space with no distractions

Chapter 3

Schedules

There are many types of schedules that can be used with children with autism. It is important to understand the usefulness of schedules and how they can help to make the process of completing work tasks easier for an individual with autism. In fact, schedules help the process of completing work tasks for all of us, as many of us use checklists, scheduled lunch breaks at work, to do lists, scheduled days off, and more to help us make it through the work day. Schedules help make the routine more predictable and manageable for most individuals with autism. The following pages mention a few types of schedules.

<u>Individual Schedules</u>

Individual or personal schedules can take many forms. They are needed to help people organize and learn routines. In addition, they can help some children tolerate changes in routine. Individual or personal schedules build predictability into the lives of children with autism and may relieve stress for other children with autism by giving them an idea of what to expect. Many children will begin to develop independent skills for monitoring their daily activities by using schedules.

Please understand that these schedules may take some time to develop. You will first have to see several types of schedules to know which type you like or which type you feel will be appropriate for your child. Try providing yourself with visual samples of schedules by doing an internet image search for "autism visual schedules."

One key similarity in all individual schedules is that they all have a finished component, in which the child symbolizes that an activity is completed. As my mentor once advised me, students *need to be taught how* to use their schedules. They may require most-to-least (provide assistance, then fade the assistance) prompting and physical guidance for a while. Regardless of the prompting, individual or personal schedules are made to fit the specific needs and abilities of the child and these schedules would use real objects, pictures, icons or words depending on what the child can relate to the best.

Making Schedules

To make schedules, people use a variety of methods and styles until they find one that works for the child. The easiest way to get started is to laminate a sheet of paper or a folder. Then, use Velcro ™ to secure the pictures. Be sure to keep the Velcro consistent (ex. Always stick the "fuzzy" side on the item that stays put and use the rough side for the items that are removed from the schedule or vice versa.) Foam board is another great material to use for schedules because it is already sturdy and immediately ready for use. It can be found at any office supply store or craft store.

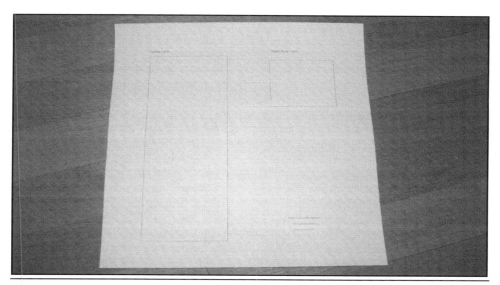

A file folder schedule template. The current activity goes in the box on the right. The upcoming activities are lined up in the box on the left. The finished items are placed in a bag at the bottom or on the inside of the folder.

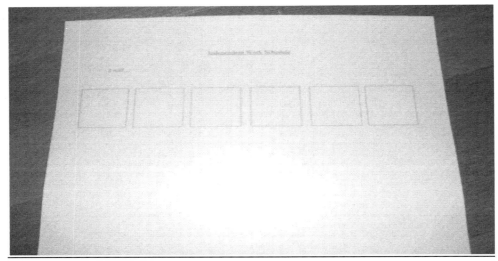

A task schedule template. The picture icons are placed in the order that the tasks will be done (inside the squares). Be sure to include a picture icon of the reward or item that the child will receive for completing the work.

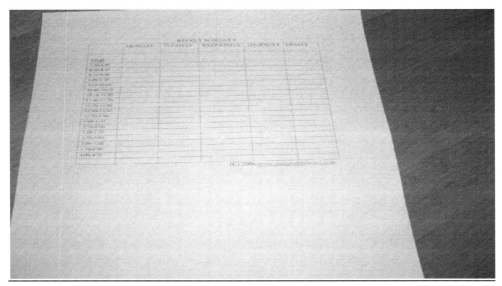

A weekly schedule template. This schedule will help the adult to show the planned activities for the week.

A hanging/mounted picture schedule. (Picture symbols from Mayer-Johnson's Boardmaker software.) The pocket on the bottom is for the activities that are completed.

Task Schedules

Task schedules, also called mini-task schedules (Hodgdon, 1995) could be thought of as directions. They help to visually "break-down" a task or an activity. Task schedules show a child what will occur within the context of a structured lesson or activity, much like directions. Task schedules can also help children perform tasks without the use of a verbal prompt from the adult. This can increase independence. They are used to give children a visual cue of what is expected. Task schedules are helpful throughout the day. They also should be created based on the child's ability level and they will take time to create. To start with, you may want to create task schedules for routine activities that you have frequently such as washing hands, cleaning a room, play time and work time. The task schedule could to be made using a sturdy board, like foam board or cardstock, and can have detachable icons, photos or objects. If it is an activity that will occur infrequently, it is sometimes easier to make a quick task schedule on a piece of paper or index card.

Task Schedule for a child to get dressed after swimming class…

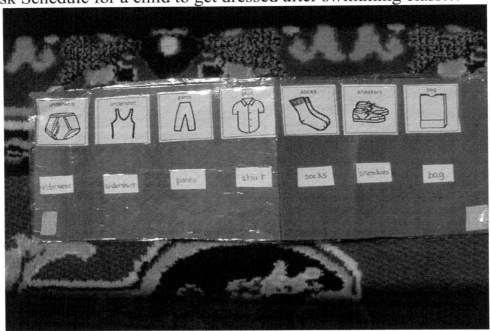

Task Schedule for a child to complete a chore…

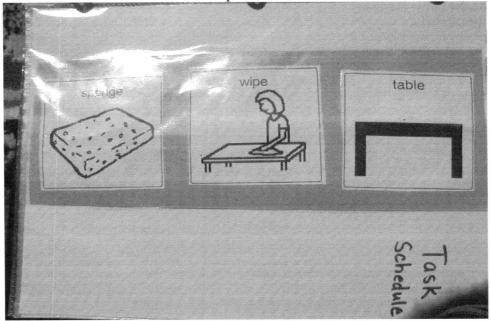

Task Schedule for cleaning up after an activity...

Self- Monitored Work Schedules

Self-Monitored work schedules help children to manage their time. Based on the TEACCH (Treatment and Education of Autistic and related Communication-Handicapped Children) methodology, they are used to promote independent task completion and to decrease the need for adult intervention. These types of schedules tell the child exactly what work activity is required of them during the independent work/self-monitored work session, how much they are responsible for completing and when they will be finished. Self-Monitored work schedules can be created in many different ways. Some people use a binder and plastic sleeves to showcase the tasks, while others use a folder with the tasks mounted to the front. These visual schedules should be sure to indicate any break times during the self-monitored work session. Self-Monitored work schedules should include a finished component so that child can indicate when their work is complete. The book Activity Schedules for Children with Autism by McClannahan & Krantz (1998) offers many good examples and detailed strategies for creating work or activity schedules.

Break Schedule (when needed)

These schedules give the child a visual indicator of when their reinforcement, preferred item, or break will occur. These may be helpful for a child who has behavior intervention plan and needs to be reminded that their reinforcement will be coming soon. The visual support is helpful for many people.

Chapter 4

Data Collection & Measuring Progress

Data Collection is an important tool in measuring the progress towards objectives. It can also let you know if your teaching method or intervention is effective or not. Most often, it is more effective to have data taken in the place or activity where the task is performed. This makes it easier to record accurate and reliable data. If you choose to create one, a data collection system could be a great benefit. The chart below details a few different types of data.

<u>Types of Data</u>

Frequency - number of times a behavior occurs

Duration - amount of time a behavior occurs

Latency - amount of time between the start of the opportunity and the behavior

Percent - number of occurrences out of the number of opportunities

Intensity - physical force or magnitude of response

Time Sample - observation period divided into intervals

Permanent Product - count of the behavior by observing the product

Interval Recording - recording behavior in intervals

Data sheets are needed to record data. There are various types of data sheets which can be used for any given objective. It will be important to locate several types of data sheets so that data can be accurately recorded. For instance, if you want to record the frequency of a child's aggressive behaviors, you may use a data sheet which just allows you to chart tally marks. The tally marks will show you how many times per day that behavior is occurring. To take this data collection idea a little further, if you wanted to know the times that the aggressive behavior is occurring, you may want to use a data sheet which allows for tally marks in a specific time period. Therefore, your data sheet should be more detailed. Examples are below:

Target Behavior: Hitting

///// ///// //

Morning Total= 12

	Hitting	Throwing	Biting	Attempted Biting
8:30	///	////		//
9:00	//	/////		//
9:30	///	/////	/	//
10:00	////	///		/
Morning Totals	12	17	1	7

How to Set Up a Work Area at Home for a Child with Autism

If you are trying to record progress on a task in which the child will be doing something like matching, identifying, imitating or labeling to produce a correct response, you may want to use a data sheet which will allow you to record several trials of that same task.   This type of data sheet would allow you to:

1. label the individual items the child is focusing on
2. record the child's answer for each trial

Samples of data sheets used for this purpose are below:

The child will point to the correct item when given the label.   ITEM : "SHOE"

DATE	Trial 1	Trial 2	Trial 3	Trial 4	Trial 5	%
5/1						
5/2						
5/3						
5/4						
5/5						

If you choose to use a data sheet such as this, you also may want to have a data sheet for each item the child is to match, identify, imitate or label. Having a separate data sheet is done so that you will know exactly which items on which the child is progressing. However, if you prefer another method, this next data sheet shows how you would highlight specific items on which the child is focusing, on the data sheet.

Objective: The child will point to the correct item, when given the label.

	Trial 1	Trial 2	Trial 3	Trial 4	Trial 5	Total %
Shoe	+	-	-	-	-	20%
Ball	-	+	-	-	+	40%
cookie	-	+	+	+	+	80%
coat	-	-	+	-	-	0%
crayon	-	-	+	+	+	60%

Often, it helps to have several items the child is focusing on listed on one page. This saves time and energy when you are working on a similar task, but are using different items. For example, if the child is supposed to identify colors, you may want a data sheet which allows you to chart your child's progress for three colors on one page. A sample that was shown to me by a mentor is below:

Objective: The child will identify primary colors.

ITEM: "Identify RED"

5/1	5/2	5/3	5/4	5/5														
+	-	-	+	-														
-	-	-	-	-														
+	-	-	+	+														
-	-	+	+	+														
+	-	+	+	+														
3/5	0/5	2/5	4/5	3/5														

ITEM: "Identify BLUE"

5/1	5/2	5/3	5/4	5/5														
-	-	-	+	-														
-	-	-	-	+														
-	-	-	+	+														
-	-	+	+	+														
-	-	+	+	+														
0/5	0/5	2/5	4/5	4/5														

ITEM: "Identify YELLOW"

5/1	5/2	5/3	5/4	5/5														
+	-	+	+	+														
+	-	+	+	+														
+	-	-	+	+														
+	-	+	+	+														
+	-	+	+	+														
5/5	0/5	4/5	5/5	5/5														

Another type of data sheet which is extremely helpful in charting progress is a task analysis data sheet. This type of data sheet lists all the steps in a task analysis and records the child's progress in each step. A concrete example would be a hand-washing task. During the task of hand-washing, there are several steps that the child must complete. The data sheet for this task would record how well he or she does on each of those steps. In addition, this type of data sheet indicates what type of prompt the child received.

	5/1	5/2	5/3	5/4	5/5			
Turn on Water	P	P	P	P	P			
Get Soap	P	P	P	P	P			
Run water on hands	P	P	P	P	P			
Rub in Soap	P	P	P	P	G			
Put Soap Down	G	G	G	G	I			
Rinse hands under water	P	P	P	P	P			
Turn off Water	P	P	P	P	P			
Get Paper towel	G	G	G	G	V			
Dry Hands	P	P	P	P	P			
Throw paper towel in trash	P	P	G	G	I			

Prompts Needed
I= the child completed the task independently
V= the child needed a verbal reminder to complete the task
G= the child needed a gesture or model from the adult to complete the task
P= physical assistance was needed to complete the task

Recording Data...

Anytime you record data or create a data sheet, you want to include the key. The key will tell you how to record the data. In some instances, you may only want to know if the child was correct or incorrect. In other instances, you may want to know the prompt level the child received to complete the task. In either case, always include the key on any data sheets you are using.

KEY
I= the child completed the task independently
V=the child needed a verbal reminder to complete the task
G= the child needed a gesture or model from the adult to complete the task
P=physical assistance was needed to complete the task

KEY
+ = correct
- = incorrect
NR = no response

Permanent product data sheets are data sheets in which the child's actual production of the task is right there on the paper. This type of data sheet or "work sample" allows you to actually see what the child can produce. Permanent product data sheets can be useful for documenting things like writing skills, tracing skills and coloring skills. If a child's objective is to color within a circle 4 out of 5 times, you could create a data sheet which has 5 circles and have your child color inside of them. As they complete the task you write the prompt level your child needed to complete the task directly on the paper. A sample of the data sheet is below:

Color in the Circles.

As you may see, even in these few examples, there are many ways to create data sheets. You will need to create and use data sheets which are meaningful to you, since you will be the person interpreting the data. Data sheets help by showing you exactly what skills to focus in on during your lessons.

<u>Things to Think About When Creating Data Systems:</u>

- Remember that this process will take some time.

- Make enough blank copies of each data sheet before beginning.

- You will need to first have a copy of your child's IEP or your selected personal goals and objectives.

- An individualized binder or folder which holds the child's data sheets is helpful.

- Use page dividers to separate the goals and objectives into categories in the binder or folders. (For example, imitation skills, fine motor skills, math skills, vocabulary, basic concepts, etc.)

- Discuss data collection as a team. Make sure that all family members or caregivers working with your child, know how to record the data accurately and are using the same key/symbols. Also, make sure that everyone uses the same verbal direction when asking the child to perform the task.

- Write down on the data sheet exactly what should be said to get the child to perform the task. Use simple language.

- Remember that data is often more accurate when taken in the area where the activity/task is performed. This is so you can record it immediately.

Sample blank data sheets are on the following pages:

How to Set Up a Work Area at Home for a Child with Autism

Skill to Work on:
Direction/Words to Say:

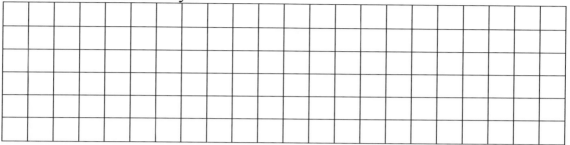

Skill to Work on:
Direction/Words to Say:

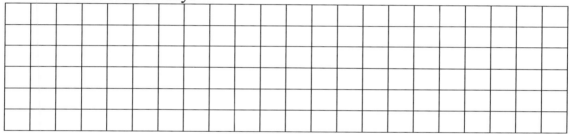

Skill to Work on:
Direction/Words to Say:

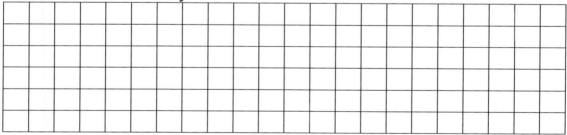

Key:
+ = correct   I= independent   V=verbal   G=gesture   PP=partial physical   FP=full physical
- = incorrect

How to Set Up a Work Area at Home for a Child with Autism

Skill to Work on:
Direction/Words to Say:

List Steps or Individual Items Below								

Key:
+ = correct   I= independent   V=verbal G=gesture   PP=partial physical   FP=full physical
- = incorrect

Frequency Data Chart

Behavior _____

Daily Total_____

Behavior _____

Daily Total_____

Behavior _____

Daily Total_____

Behavior _____

Daily Total_____

Behavior _____

Daily Total_____

Date:_____

Trace.

How to Set Up a Work Area at Home for a Child with Autism

Trace.

Trace.

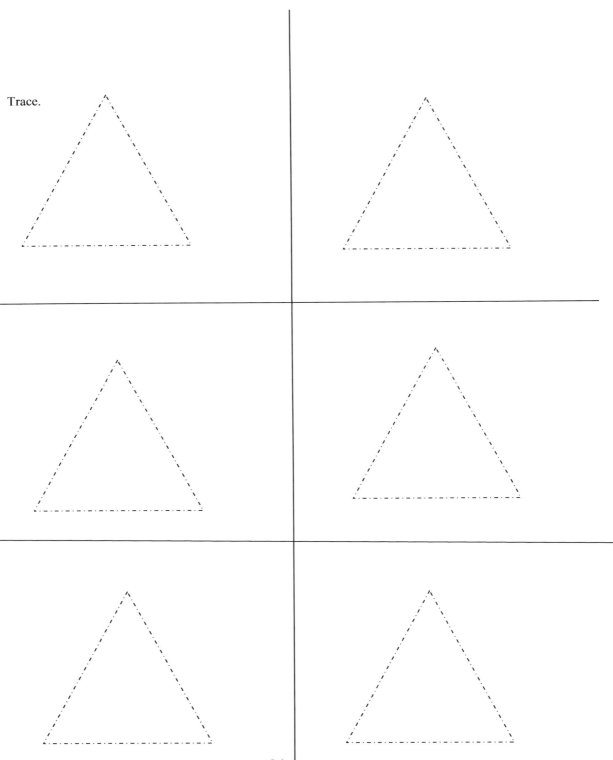

Color.

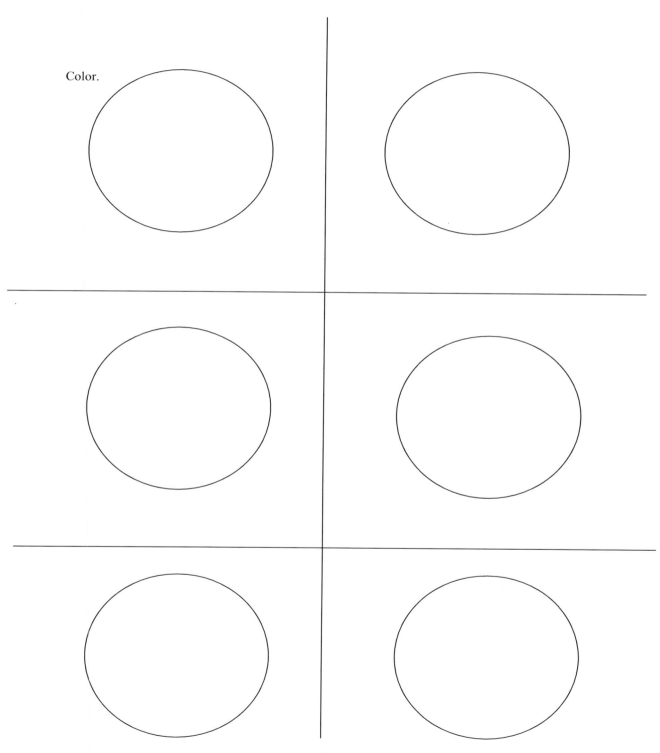

How to Set Up a Work Area at Home for a Child with Autism

Color.

26

Color.

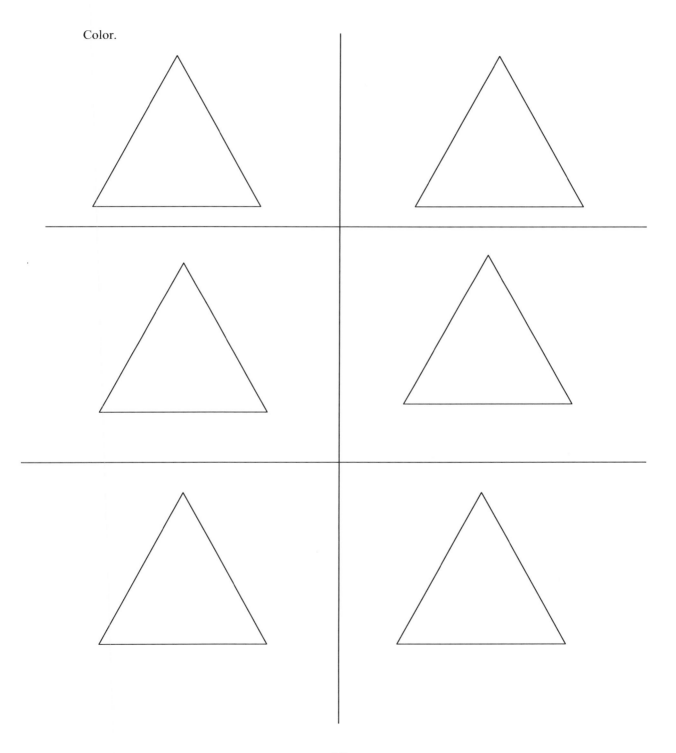

This page allows you to write any line, letter, shape, etc. and have your child imitate or copy it in the square below.

How to Set Up a Work Area at Home for a Child with Autism

29

A suggestion to teach sequential steps to drawing a horizontal line…

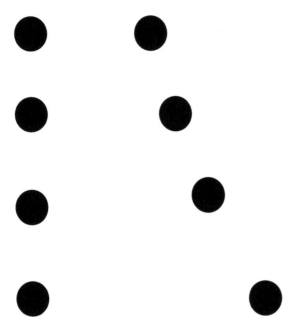

Draw a vertical line.

Draw a vertical line.

Trace the lines.

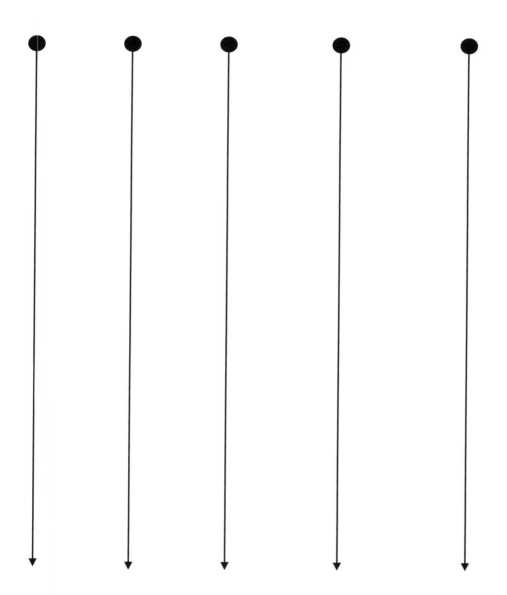

Draw a line to the sticker or candy. (Parents, place your child's favorite stickers or small candy or cereal on the bottom circle.)

●   ●   ●   ●   ●

●   ●   ●   ●   ●

Chapter 5

Self-Monitored Work Tasks

Of course there are many different ways to make any given work task. We will discuss a few ways to make some work tasks with your child's independence in mind. The goal for these particular tasks is to get them to do it on their own. I know it may sound like a difficult task to some, but we might as well start now. I often hear from teachers in the classrooms that I work with "Oh, he can't work on that independently." My answer is the same each time, "Not Yet!"

The idea behind the self-monitored tasks is that during these tasks, the child will work on structured tasks by themselves (eventually) from start to finish. At first they may need much guidance from you. This activity tends to be more beneficial if the child has their own desk or work space and their own set of materials. Creating materials for this area may take some time. These specific work tasks need to be tasks that the child is already skilled at doing. The goal is to get him or her to work for an extended period of time, not to learn a new skill. Tasks should be *related* to the objectives you are working on in the Adult-Directed Tasks page 39 and they should be easy to look at, easy to understand and easy to complete, without help from the adult. Typically, the tasks should be set up to be completed in a left to right or top to bottom sequence (www.TEACCH.com). After completing work tasks, the child will need a place to store their finished work. This tends to be a place to the right of the child, such as an empty box or container, which symbolizes that the task is finished. The University of North Carolina's TEACCH program utilizes jigs (structured work tasks) for teaching independent work skills. Some really good examples of these work tasks can be found on AutismClassroom.com's Parent Page under the caption "Self-monitored Work Tasks."

The self-monitored work schedules are ideal for use in this setting. A visual symbol, such as a photo, object or a picture icon, to tell the child what task to work on next, will be needed. The picture, object or photo, can be placed on a laminated piece of paper or in a binder with plastic sleeves. Each page could hold description of what is to be done.

Self-monitored work task usually are presented in a fashion that answers the following 4 questions (http://www.specialed.us/autism/structure/str12.htm) for the child:

1. What is the work to be done? 2. How much is to be done?
3. When am I finished? 4. What comes next?

Tips for Self-Monitoring Work Tasks

- Remember, these particular work tasks will be hands-on activities designed to have the child learn to be productive and independent. They will be different from adult directed lessons that teach new concepts. These tasks will reinforce known concepts.

- Collect various containers of different sizes with lids. Empty bins or corrugated boxes work well too.

- Velcro ™ works well for keeping materials grounded.

- Check the dollar store for materials to make the tasks.

- Large storage bins can help to hold your child's work tasks.

- Photos or icons of the tasks may help to show which work task to complete.

- Use an icon to show "finished" or "reinforcer" when they are done.

- Start with having the child complete one small task, then provide him or her with a reinforcer item or toy. Gradually work up to adding more tasks.

- Tasks Galore, by Laurie Eckenrode, Pat Fennell, and Kathy Hearsey is a book filled front to back with self-monitored work task ideas and pictures.

- Provide only physical prompts, no verbal comments for completing the work tasks, since the goal is to get them to complete the task without the verbal prompting from the adult. Gradually decrease the physical prompts as time goes on (McClannahan &. Krantz, 1998). The Activity Schedules book by McClannahan &. Krantz, provides more information on the topic of self-monitored work tasks.

A Few Sample Pictures of Self-Monitored Work Tasks

Matching colored hearts.

Sorting by shape.

Matching colors.

ABC matching.

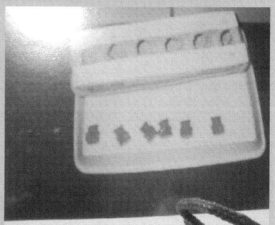

Fine Motor Practice (placing counting bears into an egg carton)

Self-monitored tasks can take various forms, such as folding laundry and washing dishes. However, for the sake of this book, we will describe self-monitored tasks which will be specifically for table top or desk top use. They will be those that a child would use while sitting down or standing at a table, during a work period. Self-monitored tasks are usually created using a sturdy foundation such as a cardboard box, soda case boxes, shoeboxes, boxes that hold candy, sturdy trays, or any other material that can hold up to a child! The materials added to the inside of the task are typically fastened down with Velro™ or tape, except for those materials that might be sorted, categorized or manipulated in some way.

The typical types of items that are added to the tasks, include materials that **may** emphasize:

- sorting
- counting
- fine motor skills
- opening
- eye-hand coordination
- matching
- labeling
- reading
- letter and number recognition
- picture identification
- recognizing shapes or puzzles
- file folder games
- and, whatever you want to work on…

The **few** typical types of basic skills the child may be working on include:

- putting counting bears into a container
- using a pincer grasp to take clothespins off of a container
- matching a colored bear to a corresponding color
- placing the picture with the beginning letter
- taking two pieces of a hair curler and snapping together
- collating or sorting papers
- placing clothes pins on stickers on an index card
- and, whatever you want to work on…

Chapter 6

Adult Directed Work Tasks

Adult Directed Work Tasks will be those tasks in which you are teaching your child a new skill. These tasks will be identified by you or the school team, based on your child's needs. For the skills that can be taught at a table or desk, try some of the strategies in this chapter. When thinking about what skills to target or to work on, it is often helpful to first take a look at where your child is currently functioning. There are many formal assessment tools for measuring skill levels which are used in the school systems and by consultants. However, we will discuss informal assessment measures. If you have up to date assessment information from the school system or another agency, use that. If not, try this method. Simply write a list of 10-12 specific skills that your child has. Then, write another list of 10-12 specific skills you would like for your child to learn. Next, take a look at a developmental milestones chart. A developmental milestones chart can be found at any one of the following websites or you can find a developmental milestones chart by doing an internet search for the term.

http://www.pbs.org/wholechild/abc/index.html
http://www.nidcd.nih.gov/health/voice/
http://www.reachoutandread.org/about_develop.html

This will be important so that you can be sure that the skills you want your child to learn are age appropriate and in a good developmental sequence. You don't want a 2 year old to work on something that a 5 year old can't even do. Next, find a middle ground between the skills your child is already showing and the skills you want your child to learn. Use that middle ground as the starting point for the at home lessons. For example, if your child can already match items by color, maybe the next step could be to have them begin to identify colors when you ask them to. Another example is, if your child can make circular scribbles on paper, maybe you could have them begin to work on drawing horizontal and vertical lines. Or, if your child has a skill of picking up items, maybe they could begin to learn a sequence for cleaning up their room. Whatever the skill, be very specific when describing what you want your child to do. A few ideas for choosing skills to focus on are below.

Some Beginning Ideas for Skills to Look For or Work On:
(Source: Behavioral Intervention for Young Children with Autism by Maurice, Green and Luce)

- Imitating movements, (physical movements, movements or writing using hands, mouth movements)
- Identifying body parts, objects, pictures, people, action words, functions of objects, sounds, big/small, tall/short, colors, family member's pictures, places, etc.
- Feeding self, use of a straw, dressing or undressing self, cleaning face after eating
- Matching colors, pictures, objects to objects, picture to picture, picture to object, numbers to quantities, etc.
- Labeling (by words, signs or pictures) objects, pictures, photos, numbers, letters
- Imitating phrases, answering to "What is your name?"

Finally, create a teaching plan for each skill you have chosen. Each skill/goal/objective should be very specific in describing what you want your child to do. For example, it would be better to say you want your son or daughter to identify the colors blue, red, yellow and brown, rather than to say you want them to "learn their colors." Having a specific target will help you to channel your teaching and move to the next level once those specific goals or skills have been accomplished. Having a teaching plan may help to make this process a little easier. Some sample teaching plans are listed for you on the next few pages.

****The teaching plan should include the following elements.****

-*The Skill to be Learned*
-*Materials Needed*
-*Plan to Make the Materials*
-*Ideas for Data Collection*
-*Teaching Technique to be Used*
-*Motivator/Preferred Item/Reinforcer*

TEACHING PLAN SAMPLE #1

Skill- John will identify the colors red, yellow, blue and green, by putting the color in my hand.

Materials Needed- Identical cards, blocks, toys or manipulatives that differ only by color.

Plan to Make the Materials- Find Pre-made items.

Ideas for Data Collection-Create a data sheet for each color or use a sheet that allows progress charting for several colors on one page.

Teaching Technique to be Used-Work on teaching one color at a time until it is mastered. Present one color and ask John to put it in my hand. Help him to do it. Reward John with his preferred item. After about 5 successes with one color at a time, present John with the same color and one distracter color. Ask him to give the initial color requested. Follow this pattern for the other colors.

Preferred Item/Reinforcer – Thomas the Tank Engine Toy or Slinky toy.

TEACHING PLAN SAMPLE #2

Skill- Santiago will cut 6 inch lines.

Materials Needed- Child scissors, index cards cut in ½ inch strips.

Plan to Make the Materials- Draw a line down the blank side of the index card (for about 4 cards). Cut index cards into ½ inch strips.

Ideas for Data Collection-Create a data sheet for recording Santiago's attempts.

Teaching Technique to be Used-Help Santiago cut ½ inch strips at first. Reward him for each strip he cuts. Gradually increase the length to 1 inch, 1 ½ inches, 2 inches, etc.

Preferred Item/Reinforcer – Tickles and a deep pressure sensory activity.

Teaching Plan
(photocopy as you wish)

Skill-

_____

_____

_____

Materials Needed-

_____

_____

_____

Plan to Make the Materials-

_____

_____

_____

Ideas for Data Collection-

_____

_____

_____

Teaching Technique to be Used-

_____

_____

_____

Motivators/Preferred Items/Reinforcers-

_____

_____

Once you have decided what to teach, it will be important to begin to gather the materials to help you teach. To begin organizing your materials for the adult directed tasks, here are some tips.

<u>Organizing your Materials</u>

- Zipper-type baggies are helpful for storing your child's individual materials and reinforcers/preferred items. Try purchasing several sizes from extra small to jumbo.   They will always come in handy.

- Create one labeled baggie for each objective you will be working on in a 1:1 desk top setting. (For example, bathroom goals or mealtime objectives would not fit in to this category. However, matching, sorting and identifying items may work well in this area.) Store the materials for each objective in their own baggie.

- Use a permanent marker to write the specific goal or objective on the baggie. This will help you to keep the correct items in the correct bag.

- Make a reinforcer box or container for your child which has a variety of about 6 or 7 reinforcers or preferred items chosen specifically for him or her. **These selected reinforcers will be most effective if your child is only allowed access to them during work times and not at other times.**

- Limit distractions by selecting work areas near a blank wall or in areas with limited visual distractions (www.TEACCH.com). If there is not blank wall, place a curtain, a screen, or plain fabric up to create a blank space.

Some Ideas for Teaching Basic Skills:

TEACHING WRITING SKILLS

1. Remember that this task can be difficult at times due to sensory challenges which can make holding a writing instrument difficult.

2. Try your best to use the proper development sequence for writing skills.

3. Use most to least prompts (ex. Hand over hand assistance to help to always get it correct, then gradually reduce the assistance, as your child writes better.)

4. Make it fun. (Ex. Use toy animals as pencils, have the child draw a line to their favorite candy or cereal.)

5. Make multi-sensory writing opportunities (Ex. Writing in shaving cream, pudding, whipped cream or using sand paper letters.)

TEACHING SCISSOR SKILLS

1. Start with making snips in paper.

2. Move to small pieces of heavy cardstock or index card paper about 1/2 inch or 1 inch.

3. Increase the paper size gradually.

4. Encourage "cutting on the line."

5. Move to shapes in a sequenced order (Ex. When first teaching to cut a square, have all parts of the square pre-cut except one side. Then move to having all parts of the square pre-cut except for 2 sides, etc.

Some Ideas for Teaching Basic Skills:

TEACHING DRESSING SKILLS

1. First find out if your child can first remove clothing when asked.

2. Use oversized clothing (adult sized sweat pants and sweatshirt) to teach the skill on a daily basis. Have them practice over their own clothes.

3. Use the least amount of physical prompting necessary.

4. Use visual supports such as pictures or directions for the dressing sequence.

5. Break down tasks into small parts and consider your child's strengths.

TEACHING BASIC CONCEPT SKILLS

1. Present 1 or 2 items at a time. For example, if you are teaching colors or numbers, don't teach eight colors at once. Start with one or two until your child masters the objectives/goals, then move on to another color, then another, etc.

2. Clear the table off, except for what you are trying to get your child to focus on.

3. When you first start, make the correct answer stand out (Ex. If teaching the shape "circle," try using a large circle and a small square. Gradually, switch to shapes that are the same size.)

4. When starting to teach concepts or attributes, be sure to keep all elements of the materials the same except for the attribute you are working on (Ex. If you are teaching colors, have items which are exactly the same except for the color. If you are teaching shapes, have shapes which are exactly the same color, but differ only in shape.)

5. Teach more difficult vocabulary identification tasks, by first having your child match the picture, number or word to the exact same picture number or word. Next, you provide the vocabulary for what they are matching as you give them the picture (Ex. "match dog," "match book," "match number 2"). Gradually, begin to ask them to give you the picture, number or word (Ex. "give dog" "give book" "give number 2.")

During Adult-Directed Tasks, various teaching methods can be used. The following pages provide information about only a few teaching methods. But before you begin teaching, you will need to find motivators for your child. With either method or methods, you choose, in order to increase learning and motivation, you will want to use reinforcers or preferred items that your child will communicate for or work for. **Without a highly motivating item, you may have a difficult time getting your child to do the task**. Utilizing preferred items to help motivate the child to work on the task is important. Choosing preferred items that are appropriate will greatly influence their impact.

When Choosing Motivators, Try the Following Ideas:

- present a variety of items to your child
- take notice of what items your child reaches for, asks for or avoids
- remember motivators and reinforcers can be <u>anything</u> your child finds reinforcing, not just what you think they should like
- tangible items (ex.toy, radio, magazine, etc.)
- edible items (ex. *extra small* amounts of food or candy, etc.)
- sensory items (ex. tickles, lotion, auditory/music, etc.)
- activities (ex. peek-a-boo, songs, break time, etc.)
- social attention (ex. praise, high fives, etc.)

A Few Teaching Techniques from Various Internet and Book Sources

ABA(Applied Behavior Analysis) (from www.Kathyandcalvin.com)

Applied Behavior Analysis (ABA) is the science of human behavior and learning that began even before the work of B.F. Skinner over 70 years ago. Skinner taught us that learning can be accelerated by arranging the learning environment and consequences of behavior in classrooms. Teachers or parents who actively work to organize the learning environments of their students to accelerate learning are more effective than those teachers who instead rely on the student to organize his environment.

Through many years of research in the field of ABA, we have learned that the important parts of the learning environments that we need to organize are:

1. What we do to make a behavior occur.

2. What we do after the behavior occurs to make it stronger in the future. In other words, if we want a child with autism to learn to come to us every time we call him then we have to

    -do something to make the behavior occur (call him) and then

    -do something after the behavior that will make him want to come next time (give a reinforcer or a reward. This process of arranging antecedents (calling) and consequences (giving a reinforcer) is the basic unit of all teaching for children with autism. If you learn how to arrange these antecedents and consequences you will teach your student/child many skills.

DTT (Discrete Trial Training) (from www.polyxo.com)

A discrete trial is a form of Applied Behavior Analysis. It is a method for teaching a new skill. It involves breaking down a lesson into small parts. A discrete trial is a single cycle of a behaviorally-based instruction routine. A particular trial may be repeated several times in succession, several times a day, over several days (or even longer) until the skill is mastered. There are four parts, and an optional fifth, to a discrete trial.

- the **discriminative stimulus** (S^D)-- the instruction or environmental cue to which the adult would like the child to respond

- the **prompting stimulus** (S^P)-- a prompt or cue from the adult to help the child respond correctly (optional)

- the **response** (R)-- the skill or behavior that is the target of the instruction

- the **reinforcing stimulus** (S^R)-- a reward designed to motivate the child to respond and respond correctly

- the **inter-trial interval** (^{ITI})-- a brief pause between consecutive trials

Tips for Conducting a Discrete Trial

1. *A general protocol for dealing with difficult behaviors during a Discrete Trial would be to block (stop) the child from engaging in the behavior & focus on the task, do not mention the inappropriate behavior, just mention the task to be completed. However, if there is another specific behavior plan for a child, follow the child's plan.*
2. *Remove all distractions from the work area.*
3. *Use motivators and preferred items for your child to work for.*
4. *When presenting choices, usually (not always) present only 2 or 3 items at a time.*

Errorless Learning (from www.christinaburkaba.com)

Errorless Learning is a method of teaching in which the learner is prompted to get the correct answer. It is a most-to-least prompting method. The learner learns through repeated trials using prompts. Prompts are then faded at a rate in which the learner continues to stay successful. The learner is reinforced for success and tends to stay more motivated to complete the task. Errorless Learning is appropriate to use whenever teaching a new skill. It is also important in the beginning stages of learning when trying to establish instructional control with a child.

No- No Prompting (from www.christinaburkaba.com)

No-No Prompting is technique in which least to most prompts are used. The student is given the opportunity to choose the answer, (whether right or wrong), and then is corrected (by the adult saying "no") and the student is prompted to the correct answer. Some people believe that this method can sometimes lead to a child developing an incorrect chain of responding.

Direct Instruction

Direct instruction is 1:1 interaction where the student is introduced to a concept/skill, practices the skill, and demonstrates comprehension of the skill. During direct instruction, use specific, broken-down steps to teach the skill. Next, provide opportunities for the practice. Then, attempt to have the child demonstrate the concept/skill independently and in other settings.

Applied Verbal Behavior/Verbal Behavior Intervention

Verbal Behavior Intervention is a form of Applied Behavioral Analysis (ABA) based on B.F. Skinner's book Verbal Behavior. Verbal Behavior Intervention addresses communication difficulties in individuals with autism. Skinner concluded that there are various verbal operants which each serve a different function. This method emphasizes functional language and a use of motivating items to encourage communication.

Verbal Behavior terms (from http://www.autismusaba.de/english.html):
- **Mand:** Requesting wants and needs
- **Tact:** Labeling or describing objects
- **Receptive repertoire:** Non-verbally following directions, discriminating between pictures and objects
- **Imitation:** Repeating, copying what was observed
- **Echoic:** Vocal imitation
- **Intraverbal:** Verbally (or using sign language) responding to the verbal behavior of others
- **Textural:** reading
- **Transcriptive:** Writing

Shaping (Miltenbereger, 1997)

This method is used to develop a target behavior that the child **does not** currently have. Shaping is "differential reinforcement of successive approximation of a target behavior until the behavior is exhibited by the individual." Essentially, shaping helps to reinforce the baby steps the child makes until the attempts have grown closer to the target behavior.

To begin shaping:

- To begin shaping, you identify a behavior that the child is already doing that is an approximation of the target behavior (the behavior you want from the child). This is called the starting behavior or first approximation.
- You reinforce this starting behavior and as a result, the child starts to exhibit this behavior more often.
- You then **stop** reinforcing the starting behavior and start reinforcing a behavior that is a little closer to the target behavior. (As a result, the child will start to do the new behavior more often (because it is reinforcing) and do the previous behavior less often.
- This process continues for closer and closer approximations until the target behavior is seen. (Miltenbereger, 1997)

Shaping Example 1
- Target Behavior =wearing glasses
- Starting Behavior=cries throws glasses on the ground
- Successive Approximations (baby steps) included:
  - Touching the glasses
  - Picking up the glasses
  - Putting glasses to face
  - Putting glasses on
  - Wearing the glasses

Shaping Example 2
- Target Behavior=saying "more"
- Starting behavior=says "mmm"
- Successive Approximations (baby steps) included:
- Saying "mmm" sound
- Saying "mo"
- Saying "more"

Shaping Example 3
- Child cries and the adult gives the child a toy and talks to the child.
- Child cries, does not get a response, so the child makes a loud crashing noises, the adult comes in the room tells the child to pick up toys and talks to the child.
- Child cries, makes loud crashing noises, does not get a response, so the child screams and throws toys as well, the adult comes into the room lectures the child and places the child in time out.
- Adult is concerned because the behavior has become worse.
(In this example, the adult shaped the behavior into a full blown tantrum.)

Chaining (Miltenbereger, 1997)

The chaining method is used to teach behaviors that occur together in a sequence. There are 2 types of chaining: backward chaining and forward chaining. Backward Chaining is a technique which uses prompting and fading to teach the last behavior of the chain first. Forward Chaining is a technique in which you teach the first component, then the second component, etc.

Backward Chaining (Miltenbereger, 1997)

Backward chaining is a method that can be used with individuals with who may normally be difficult to teach. In this method, the child completes the chain (performs the last behavior in the sequence or the last part of the sequence) on every learning trial. The reinforcer follows. This method gives the child the chance to be successful in completing the task. Next, the child completes the last 2 behaviors of the chain, and then the last 3, etc.

Backward Chaining Example:
(Washing hands)
•First teach throwing paper towel away, then drying hands, then turning water off, then rinsing hands, then using soap, then turning water on, etc.
(Hanging up Coat)
•First teach placing the coat w/ the hanger on the hook, then hanging coat on hanger, then taking coat off, then un-zippering, etc.
(Getting Ready for Dinner/Setting the table)
•First teach sitting at the table, then placing the silverware on the table, then placing the dishes on the table, then placing the cup on the table, then placing the placemat on the table, etc.

Forward Chaining (Miltenbereger, 1997)

In forward chaining, you prompt the child to correctly complete the first behavior in the chain, then provide a preferred item (reinforcer) following the response. Next, fade the prompts until the child can do the first behavior by themselves. Hold your reinforcer until the child completes the first 2 behaviors of the chain, then, eventually, the first 3, first 4, etc.

Task Analysis

This method involves breaking down a task into its individual components. For example, the task of washing hands can be broken down into: turning on the water, picking up the soap, rubbing the soap on hands, placing hands under water, lathering the soap, rinsing hands, turning off water, getting a paper towel, drying hands and throwing the paper towel away.

Total Task Presentation

With this method, the entire chain of behaviors is taught as a single unit.

Picture Prompts

Picture prompts include visual representation of the task to aid in student learning. They are helpful for students who are visual learners.

Incidental Teaching (from www.autismnetwork.org)

The incidental teaching method is child centered. Child selected reinforcers are utilized. This method is conducted in the natural setting and focuses on child selected activities. Teachers arrange the environment by placing preferred toys and activities of each student within sight, but not within reach, to encourage the student to initiate teaching sessions based on preplanned learning objectives.

Incidental Teaching Example:
■Level 1- adult provides a 30- second delay when a child displays interest in an object/material.
■Level 2- adult prompts the child to ask for the object.
■Level 3- more elaborate request from adult (ex. "what's this?" or " Which doll you want?")
■Level 4- correct response modeled by the adult and the child is prompted to imitate the response. Object is then presented to the child.

Mand-Model Technique (Roger-Warren, 1980)

The mand-model technique requires the use of a request or instruction for a particular behavior. The natural environment is used. In this method, the adult is the initiator of the communication. The mand-model helps children who are poor initiators of communication exchanges.

Mand-Model Technique Sample
■Step 1-The adult provides a variety of materials in a play situation (or meal situation) to create communication opportunities.
■Step 2-When the child approaches the materials, the adult initiates the communication exchange by asking (manding) the child for a verbal request or description (ex. " What do you want?")
■Step 3-The adult provides an expansion of the mand if step 2 did not bring out the target behavior. An example would be "Show me the sign for ball" or " Say ball," while modeling the sign or word.
■Step 4-Production of the target response (following any of the above steps) results in a verbal response from the adult and the adult providing the child with the item.
■Step 5-If steps 2 or 3 fail to bring out the target behavior, the adult provides a second model , but does not expect a verbal result.
I would add, however, you can possibly prompt, sign or use picture icons, with the least amount of assistance possible.

Time Delay (Noonan & McCormick, 1993)

Time delay is used to teach children to initiate verbal interaction. It has been used successfully to increase speech in students with autism (Ingenmey and Van Houten, 1991). Sometimes time delay is called a delayed prompt.

Time Delay Technique Sample
■Step 1-Adult recognizes a situation in which the child wants an item, then waits for the child to initiate a response.
■Step 2-If the child does not respond appropriately, another delay is used.
■Step 3-If this is unsuccessful, the adult will use the mand-model procedure.

Interrupted Behavior Chain (IBC) (Mirenda and Iacona, 1988).

This method uses naturally occurring routines for communication instruction related to requests for assistance by students, who are minimally motivated to communicate (Mirenda and Iacona, 1988). In the IBC method, the instruction is given after the student begins an activity. The activity is interrupted by the adult and the student must communicate in order to have the activity continue.

Interrupted Behavior Chain Sample 1:
■During structured play activities, the child's interaction with the toy can be interrupted by having the adult take the toy away.
■When this occurs, the child can be prompted to request "car" by signing, talking or picture icon.

Interrupted Behavior Chain Sample 2:
(Non-Verbal Student)
■Student finishes swimming. The next activity is recess. The student gets the shoe, puts the shoe on and is interrupted by the teacher, who presents a picture icon that says "help."
■The student must touch the picture icon to complete the chain (get shoe tied) before going outside.

Stimulus Shaping/Prompting (Browder, 2001)

Stimulus shaping appears to be a highly successful way to teach discrimination skills. In stimulus shaping, the visual presentation of the stimuli is gradually changed over trials so that discrimination is at first easy, and then gradually more difficult. For example, when first teaching the shape of a circle, maybe the circle (which you want the child to choose) can be three times larger than the other shape. Then eventually, make it smaller so that it is the same size as the other shape.

Stimulus Fading (Browder, 2001)

Stimulus fading is the gradual removal of a prompt. This method is used to increase independence. For example, when teaching sight words, you might have a picture of the word and the written word. Then gradually, a little at a time, fade out the picture, leaving just the written word.

Response Prompt

A prompt that is presented to cue the child to perform a specific behavior.

Other Communication Techniques

- Make Items Inaccessible (have the child ask for items)
- Functional Communication Training (Teach communication in a functional/contextual way. For example, instead a child hitting to relay the message "I want attention," teach the child to say "Play with me" or to give a picture icon that says "Play with me.")
- Provide Structured Routines
- Visually Clarify Expectations, Routines, and Tasks
- Structure Play and Leisure Activities (plan them and facilitate them)
- Provide Non-Linguistic Contingent Responses (acknowledge the child's behavior)
- Provide Linguistic Contingent Responses (verbally expand on what the child says or does)

Structured Teaching (from www.teacch.com)

The professionals at the TEACCH (Treatment and Education of Autistic and related Communication-Handicapped Children) Center out of Chapel Hill, North Carolina, have developed a method for teaching children with autism that is widely used in a variety of schools. This method is often referred to as Structured Teaching. The TEACCH website states that to "effectively teach autistic students a teacher must provide structure, i.e., set up the classroom so that students understand where to be, what to do, and how to do it, all as independently as possible." The key components of Structured Teaching are physical organization, scheduling, and teaching methods. The TEACCH team also states that the key to effectively using each of these features is individualization. "A classroom that is physically well-organized and scheduled will not benefit students unless individual student strengths and needs are considered in the planning phase." These major principles can be applied to the physical set up of the work area at home, the teaching methods you might use and the implementation of using schedules with your child. The TEACCH website has much more information for parents and families and is a recommended resource.

Chapter 7

Teaching Play Skills

Some children with autism have difficulty with developing social skills and play skills. Setting up a play area and emphasizing the instruction of social skills can be one way to help. The play area may look different in everyone's home. You have to create it to meet your child's needs. Most often, for younger children, the play area will need to be sectioned off with very clear boundaries. For older individuals, some families may choose to create a table or area of a room dedicated playing games or cards or participation in some other recreation/leisure activity. Often, in the play area, the use of topic boards, the use of age-appropriate activities, and emphasis on communication and socialization skills is taught. Play/leisure activities will need to be structured, planned and guided by the adults. For many children with autism, ***direct instruction*** of recreation/leisure and play skills is critical for their social development. While there are numerous resources out there on socialization and play skills, this page and the next page list just a few things to keep in mind while teaching play skills or trying to improve or social skills.

- Free time is a difficult concept for some children with autism.
- Remember you will have to teach play skills. They do not come naturally for many children with autism.
- Teach the play skills 1:1 first, then incorporate them into a group setting (Moyes, 1997).
- Use age appropriate games and toys to the extent possible. If a seven year old without autism likes the game, chances are, your seven year old will have some interest in it too. You may just have to modify the presentation a little.
- Find a way to make the game or activity "do-able" for him or her.
- Have fun. Your child should want to come to this play area. If you are not having fun, they are probably not having fun.

- Try something new like, roller skating (start on a rug or carpet first), tennis, baseball, t-ball, soccer or bowling.
- Follow your child's lead and comment on what he or she is interested in. Try not to get too consumed in your own idea of what play should look like. Focus on the act of attending to the same item at the same time, sharing the same space and being on the "same page", more than having him or her "play" with the toy in the exact manner for which it was made.
- If you are going to play, then play. Try not to drill your child on colors and shapes and numbers, etc. during the play time. It is okay to comment on these concepts, but keep the play fun and engaging and the opposite of work time.
- Find a method to teach the skills they need. You are the facilitator. During the beginning stages, try not to leave him/her to "play on their own."
- Read up on teaching play skills to children with autism. There are many resources on the topic and there are some systematic methods to teach play.

Books and Materials Related to Teaching Social Skills

AutismClassroom.com has a list of books and materials related to teaching socials skills and communication skills on the "Communication Techniques" page of the website.

Chapter 8

Self-Help Skills

Learning self-help skills and daily living skills are important tools for becoming more independent. Teaching self-help skills and daily living skills is essential. Making things "visual" can be its own "self-help" for some children. Visual supports for daily living skills and self-help skills of several types are needed to help children with autism understand the world around them. Visual supports include any visual item that helps a child to understand or express language. They include, but are not limited to, photos, calendars, schedules, topic boards, single icons, written lists, written words, logos, and more. This chapter highlights some visual supports which can be used to help in the area of self-help skills.

Visual schedules and/or calendars are made to fit the specific needs of the individual (ex. object, picture icon, photo, word). A visual calendar can show your child what to expect each day of the month (ex. the visit to grandma's, soccer practice days, etc.) Visual schedules and calendars help make life more predictable and can ease stress levels for some children.

Augmentative Communication Methods used for Mealtimes are another type of visual support that can assist with self-help skills. Children with autism, who have language difficulties could benefit from the use of augmentative and alternative methods for communication. Mealtimes are a highly motivating time for many children. Although your child can indicate what they want during those times through pointing and leading you to the food, it is important to encourage symbolic forms of communication. The level of communication expected will depend on your child's present skills. However, visual cues can serve as a useful tool for many children with autism (both verbal and non-verbal).

To accomplish this, try having either food logos, the food wrapper, the actual food items or drink items, photos or picture icons, of the food, that the child can choose from. Have them point to, give you, or tell you, the food or drink item before consuming it (even if they can get the item themselves). At first, you may find that he or she may protest (heavily). However, if you are consistent during mealtimes, your child will learn to use symbolic forms of communication more often, whether it be handing a picture icon, using sign language or using words. Velcro ™ to make the pictures detachable, if you need to.

Sample Breakfast Meal Time Choice Board (use pictures for non-readers)

juice	milk	cereal
oatmeal	pancakes	help
spoon	fork	finished

Self-help skills and daily living skills can be enhanced by visual supports during routine activities that your child might do each day. This area is especially important, since some children may have trouble with recall, sequencing and organizing. They may need some assistance in remembering the order of things. A visual support for routine activities may help. For example, a set of pictures showing the steps in washing their hands or a visual breakdown of the task for hanging up their belongings when they come home from school can help keep some children focused. Visual supports for routines can also help to create more independence in some children.

Sample Routine Support for a Child who Reads (use pictures for non-readers)

1. Take off your backpack.
2. Take off coat.
3. Hang up coat.
4. Take out lunch bag and put it in the kitchen.
5. Take out homework folder and put it on the table.
6. Put backpack in the closet.

Self-help in the form of managing one's own behavior, is another way that visuals supports can help teach children with autism. If you have a child with a few behavioral challenges, then this paragraph may be for you. Instead of constantly verbally reminding your child of a house rule or expectation, you can visually show them what you want them to know or to do. Visual rules for

Some Ideas for Self-Help/Daily Living Skills:

TEACHING TOILETING SKILLS

1. Have a plan and work on <u>one</u> step at a time.

2. Use visual supports (check the TEACCH.com website for ideas for toilet training.)

3. Use backward chaining (physical guidance, then reinforce the last step.)

4. Use video modeling (Ex. Model from the child's point of view. There are ways to be creative without actually showing the act of someone using the bathroom. For example, use squirt bottles and chocolate candy bars to imitate the actual act of using the bathroom.)

5. Some steps for the toileting process:
   1. Sits on toilet
   2. Urinates in toilet
   3. Wipes self
   4. Time trained
   5. Requests use of the bathroom
   6. Independent

TEACHING MEALTIME SKILLS

1. Teach the skill of using a fork and spoon (Ex. Some people opt to try a 10 second "timeout" [removal of the food] for using fingers.)

2. Teach napkin use consistently.

3. Create a boundary for your child if he/she takes others food or makes a mess during meals using a placemat or a kitchen towel.

4. Provide visual supports for communicating what your child may want to say or what you may want to tell your child during meals (remember to add comments as well, such as "this taste good" or "I don't like that."

5. Encourage your child to ask for all items he/she gets during the meal time.

Some Ideas for Self-Help/Daily Living Skills:

TEACHING DRESSING SKILLS

1. Practice the skill of putting clothes on and off by using oversized adult shirts and sweatpants that your child can place over his/her clothes so they practice daily.

2. Use visual pictures to help with this skill by hanging it in their room or dresser.

3. Make a visual task schedule of the steps involved in dressing.

4. Use the visual task schedule while working on the skill.

GOING TO THE STORE

1. Provide your child with a visual list of what they will be looking for at the store (use pictures or possibly logos from the store flyer.)

2. Keep a "travel schedule" in your car to show all the places you will go to in addition to the store. Be sure to include a picture of home so they know when you will be done.

3. Use self check-out if needed. It is sometimes faster and you can have your child participate in the activity of checking the items. (This was a tip from a co-worker.)

4. Start slow if you have to. For some people, this will mean just going into the store and going back to the car. Then try going in to the store to by 1 item, like gum, at the register, then going to the car. Next, gradually add more items to the list. If you know your child will not handle it well, please do not start with a 30-list trip to the store.

GETTING YOUR CHILD TO RESPOND

1. If you have a specific behavior plan, then follow that. Otherwise, try this technique for ***most, not all*** daily instructions: Use only a few words to make a request.

2. Give your child your request only 2 times, then, on the third request always follow through with assistance.

behavior are helpful because your child may be more likely to look at the icon or written words, than to look at an adult. This is especially true when they are upset. (We all know it can be very hard to look directly at a person when you are upset with them.) Items such as pictures, iconic symbols, a schedule of what to expect or pictures of the rules, can greatly increase appropriate behaviors in some children. Linda Hodgdon's book <u>Solving Behavior Problems in Autism</u> is a good resource in this area.

Some Ways to Promote Positive Behavior in Children During Work Times:
- Pre-made and prepared activities w/all materials present
- Limited auditory and visual distractions, limited music playing in the background
- Use visual schedules for various activities & provide visual cues along with verbal language
- Neutral voice tone /Vary your tone of voice (ex. try whispering to calm someone)
- Few/limited words to express what you want your child to do
- Gesture or model along with verbal language
- Provide highly motivating activities (after) to help the child make it through a difficult activity
- Remove known problem items before the child enters the work area
- Use positive body language- try not to stand over the child or present negative body language
- Be aware of sensory issues in the child's environment and be respectful that the sensory input may be causing a problem
- Decrease difficult tasks by decreasing in numbers (ex. instead of 7 math problems, give 3)
- Decrease the amount of time expected (ex. waiting or working)
- Decrease in difficulty or make the task easier (ex. choose a 5 piece puzzle vs. a 20-piece)
- Decrease in requirements (ex. if the child is to get dressed using 6 items, reduce to 3 items.)
- Use a timed schedule such as providing attention or a favorite item every X amount of time, for positive behaviors (ex."Every 2 minutes that you keep your hands to yourself, you get a Cheerio.")
- Social rewards, verbal praise, high fives, pats on the back, tickles, etc.
- Access to highly preferred items for positive behavior and eliminate reinforcement (stop talking about the behavior you don't want to see - talk about what you want to see) for inappropriate behaviors
- Use visual cues to show your child what reward they will get for positive behavior

Chapter 9

Transitions

Transitions can be tough for many kids. Here are some ideas to attempt to make the transition to the work area a little easier.

Easing Difficult Transitions

1. Clearly indicate when an activity is done by saying the activity is done and it is time for the next activity. Use the least amount of words you can to do this.

2. Have something your child really likes at the place where they have to transition to each time.

3. Let your child carry something or "help" you to the next activity (schedule cards, picture icons, or the materials for the lesson may work well) and establish what this item will be before the moment arrives.

4. Let your child hold something when they are sitting at the activity. (Your first goal is to have your child come to the activity, you can work on having the him or her participate later.) At first, this might be all they do.

5. Give your child a 1-2 minute warning **every time any activity is almost finished** and a visual cue (ex. picture icon which states "one minute.")

6. Physically guide (using the least amount of physical contact necessary), your child to the next activity, without giving him or her the opportunity to go to the wrong place. Holding a hand works for most of the time, although not for everyone.

7. Hold your child's hand before you make the request for them to transition so that you will decrease their opportunity to run to the wrong area.

8. Use a count-down routine or a visual count-down to show your child that an activity is coming to an end. Take each icon or object off one at a time at various times to prepare them for the end of an activity.

9. Have a topic board in each activity area for your child to communicate his wants and needs. The topic board should also include "finished" and "clean-up," so that your child is aware that a transition is about to occur.

Chapter 10

Sensory Differences

I want to start this chapter by stating, I am not an expert in the field of sensory issues. However, I think sensory differences in a child can have an impact on the work area you set up at home and a child's willingness to work there. Individuals with autism sometimes experience sensory input differently than others. When this occurs, these differences affect the child's response to the world around them, their behavior, the way in which they learn and the manner in which they relate to others (Kranowitz, 1998). When people think of the senses, we typically think of five senses; sight, smell, taste, touch and hearing. When discussing sensory issues with children with autism, we must also include two other senses which are the vestibular sense and the proprioceptive sense. The vestibular sense allows your body to understand where and how it is moving in space; It is responsible for a person's balance and movement from the neck, eyes and body (Kranowitz, 1998). The proprioceptive system refers to the sense in our body which tells us about body awareness and body position perceived through our muscles, joints, ligaments, tendons and connective tissue (Kranowitz, 1998).

When interacting with your child, some of you may notice that your child may seem to over react or under react to some sensory input in one of these seven areas. Both of which could possibly affect his or her behavior. Sometimes sensory issues can make it difficult for a child to concentrate or to tolerate a particular smell, sound or sight. The behavior they may use to avoid that smell, sound or sight, may be misconstrued by the adult as defiance, when in fact, there may be a sensory issue they are trying to avoid. It is a good idea to talk with an Occupational Therapist to get professional advice regarding sensory issues. They are the experts in this area. They can give you strategies to help a child to calm, organize and focus themselves throughout the day. My goal is just to provide you with some information to get you thinking about sensory differences. Please use this information only as a beginning step to learning more about sensory differences in some people with autism. As you learn more by reading about sensory differences and talking with an Occupational Therapist, you will be better equipped to provide sensory input to your child before, during and after the work activity.

On the next page, there is a chart highlighting some of signs that may indicate to you that your child is experiencing sensory input differently. The information is only a portion of indicators that could be present. Each section lists the indicators you might see if a child is either over-responsive or under-responsive to that particular sensory input. In the chart, over-responsive reactions and under-responsive reactions are not separated. It will be useful information to know what sensory input your child seems to like, enjoy or need and what input your child avoids or does not like.

The information in this table was obtained from the book The Out of Sync Child by Carol Stock Kranowitz (1998). This book is highly recommended.

Sensory Area	Possible Indicators
Touch	• Fearful, anxious or aggressive when touched lightly or unexpectedly • Becomes afraid when touched from behind or by someone or something they are not able to see • Avoids or dislikes playing in sand, mud, water, glue, foam, etc. • Will not wear clothes with certain textures • Picky eater • Seeks out touch, appears to need to touch everything and everyone • Is not aware of being touched or bumped • Puts objects in mouth often
Vision	• Easily distracted by visual stimuli in the room (ex. Movement, decorations) • Does not make or makes limited eye contact • Notices details or patterns and not the larger picture • Difficulty finding differences in pictures, words, symbols or objects
Hearing	• Distracted by sounds that do not typically affect others (ex. Humming of lights or refrigerators, fans or clocks) • Startled by loud or unexpected sounds • Might put hands over ears • Does not answer when name is called • Listens to excessively loud music or TV
Smell	• Unusual response to smells which don't bother others • May not eat certain foods due to smell • Irritated by strong scents • Difficulty discriminating unpleasant odors • Fails to pay attention to unpleasant odors
Taste	• Picky eater • Prefers to eat hot or cold foods • Puts objects in mouth often • Drools a lot
Proprioceptive	• Likes jumping and crashing activities • Enjoys being wrapped tight in weighted blankets • May hit, bump or push others often • Uses too little or too much force with objects • Difficulty catching self if falling
Vestibular	• Avoids moving playground equipment • Afraid of having feet leave the ground • Does not like rapid or rotating movement • Constantly moving • Could spin for hours and does not appear dizzy • Seeks out fast, spinning and intense movement

Chapter 12

Resources

I hope the information in this book has been helpful to you in your efforts to set up or enhance your work area in your home. This information was meant to be a starting point for you. I encourage you to continue your efforts for teaching strategies through reading, using AutismClassroom.com's free online training materials, and by learning from your child.

For your convenience, free teaching materials such as blank forms of schedules, topic boards, task schedules, routine sequences, data sheets, colors charts, number charts, days of the week, months of the year, and other visual supports are available online at the www.autismclassroom.com website. AutismClassroom.com also has an interactive message board for parents, a sensory resources page and a page dedicated to exploring dietary concerns in children with autism. For teachers, para-professionals and administrators, AutismClassroom.com offers two other book resources: How to Set Up a Classroom for Students with Autism and Functional Behavior Assessments & Behavior Intervention Plans. For more information about the books and resources, go to www.autismclassroom.com.

References

The following books and websites have been useful in creating this book. They are listed below:

Bondy, Andy & Frost, Lori (2002). A Picture's Worth: Pecs and Other Visual Communication Strategies in Autism. Woodbine House.

Browder, Diane M. (2001). Curriculum and Assessment for Students with Moderate and Severe Disabilities. Guilford Press.

Bruce, Stephen & Gurdin, Lisa Selznick & Savage, Ron (2006). Strategies for Managing Challenging Behaviors of Students with Brain Injuries. Lash and Associates Publishing.

Hodgdon, Linda (2001). Solving Behavior Problems in Autism: Improving Communication with Visual Strategies. Quirk Roberts Publishing.

Hodgdon, Linda (1995). Visual Strategies for Improving Communication: Practical Supports for School and Home. QuirkRoberts Publishing.

Ingenmey, R., & Van Houten, R. (1991). Using time delay to promote spontaneous speech in an autistic child. Journal of Applied Behavior Analysis, 24, 591-596.

Linton, S. B. (2009). How to Set Up a Classroom for Students with Autism. AutismClassroom.com

Maurice, Green and Luce (1996). Behavioral Intervention for Young Children with Autism. Pro-Ed.

McClannahan, Lynn & Krantz, Patricia (1999). Activity Schedules for Children with Autism: Teaching Independent Behavior. Woodbine House.

Miltenbereger, Raymond G. (1997). Behavior Modification: Principles and Procedures. Wadsworth.

Moyes, Rebecca (2002). Addressing Challenging Behaviors in High Functioning Autism and Asperger's Syndrome. London: Jessica Kingsley Publishers Ltd.

Noonan, M. J., & McCormick, L. (1993). Early intervention in natural environments: methods and procedures. Pacific Grove, CA: Brooks/Cole.

Rogers-Warren, A., & Warren, S. F. (1980). Mands for verbalization. Behavior Modification, 4, 361-382.

Stock Kranowitz, Carol (2006). The Out-of-Sync Child: Recognizing and Coping with Sensory Processing Disorder. Penguin Group (USA).

www.autismclassroom.com
www.autismnetwork.org
www.autismusaba.de/english.html
www.Kathyandcalvin.com
www.cdc.gov
www.christinaburkaba.com
www.iancommunity.org
www.mayerjohnson.com
www.polyxo.com
www.specialed.us/autism/assist/asst10.htm
www.teacch.com
www.usevisualstrategies.com

About the Author:

S. B. Linton has worked with children with autism for over 10 years. She has a Master's Degree in Teaching Students with Severe Disabilities and a Graduate Certificate in Autism Spectrum Disorders from Johns Hopkins University. Linton's undergraduate degree is in Special Education from Bloomsburg University of Pennsylvania. Linton is the author of two other books: How to Set Up a Classroom for Students with Autism and Functional Behavior Assessments & Behavior Intervention Plans. Linton is the founder and manager of the AutismClassroom.com website, which provides autism information and materials for parents and educators. She currently works as an Autism Instructional Specialist and consults with school teams in matters related to teaching students with autism.

Made in the USA
Lexington, KY
15 February 2011